PARANORMAL
INVESTIGATIONS

Bigfoot, the Loch Ness Monster,

and Unexplained Creatures

Matt Bougie

Cavendish
Square

New York

Published in 2018 by Cavendish Square Publishing, LLC
243 5th Avenue, Suite 136, New York, NY 10016

Library of Congress Cataloging-in-Publication Data

Names: Bougie, Matt, author.
Title: Bigfoot, the Loch Ness monster, and unexplained creatures /
Matt Bougie.
Description: New York : Cavendish Square Publishing, 2018. |
Series: Paranormal investigations | Includes bibliographical references and index.
Identifiers: LCCN 2017000842 (print) | LCCN 2016051659 (ebook) |
ISBN 9781502628473 (library bound) | ISBN 9781502628480 (E-book)
Subjects: LCSH: Sasquatch--Juvenile literature. | Loch Ness monster--Juvenile
literature. | Cryptozoology--Juvenile literature.
Classification: LCC QL89.2.S2 (print) | LCC QL89.2.S2 B687 2018 (ebook) |
DDC 001.944--dc23
LC record available at https://lccn.loc.gov/2017000842

Editorial Director: David McNamara
Editor: Kristen Susienka
Copy Editor: Rebecca Rohan
Associate Art Director: Amy Greenan
Designer: Joseph Macri
Production Coordinator: Karol Szymczuk

Printed in the United States of America

Contents

Dragons are among the most famous paranormal creatures. They appear in many different cultural tales.

A Brief History of the Paranormal and Cryptozoology

Since prehistory, humans have tried to explain the seemingly unexplainable. Natural disasters, thunderstorms, life, death—all of these have enthralled and fascinated humanity, and civilizations and cultures around the world have tried to create some sort of logical or mysterious explanation for them. The question remains, however: how many of those explanations are simply fiction, and how many are based in fact? Today, scientists have tested and developed many theories, **debunking** previously held beliefs. However, curious cases that science can't quite explain continue to pop up over the generations. These cases are sometimes referred to as paranormal.

Dissecting the Paranormal

The word paranormal means "outside the ordinary." This can refer to individuals, objects, apparitions, or creatures that defy our understanding of science or physics. For example: a mother demonstrates superhuman strength by pulling a car off her child; reports say a person can eat metal or has resistance to extreme cold; or many sightings claim the existence of an ape-man, like the Yeti or Sasquatch.

People dedicate their lives to searching for explanations to these occurrences. Known as paranormal investigators, they examine topics that mainstream scientists ignore, such as alien visits, folktale creatures rumored to exist in the present day, and ghosts. Some of the most exciting investigations have been conducted by those searching for the truth behind paranormal creatures.

Cryptozoology

There have been many examples of fantastical creatures in folklore and fairy tales—leprechauns, fairies, and unicorns, for instance—and there are people who have spent their lives searching for their existence in the modern world. The creatures they search for, which they refer to as **cryptids**, are often said to be hidden from view. **Cryptozoologists** hunt for these cryptids and try to find evidence that either proves or disproves their existence. Bigfoot is a famous cryptid, as is the Loch Ness Monster.

The fascination with these cryptids stems from their place within our understanding of biology. We may enjoy the fantasy of fire-breathing dragons or winged horses that carry heroes through the air, but those are mostly considered fantasies. The more realistic cryptids, those creatures that could exist given their physiology and biology, seem more plausible. After all, we're discovering new species of insects and other animals all the time. We have mapped only a fraction of the ocean floor. Giant squids had all the characteristics of a cryptid until a video of a live one was captured in 2012. Bigfoot and the Loch Ness Monster share characteristics similar to a giant squid: there's nothing about their physiology that seems impossible, and their habitat is unexplored enough to leave room for a bit of mystery.

People fear unknown creatures. This painting shows a giant squid attacking a ship.

Zener cards are one set of tools that skeptics use to test people who claim to have psychic powers.

ZENER
CARDS
◆◆◆
suitable for
TELEPATHY

But the question still remains: why do *these* cryptids specifically, and cryptids in general, interest people so much that they are willing to take on great personal expense and spend years trying to find a creature that may or may not exist? Expeditions into the wilderness are dangerous, expensive, and time consuming, so why should people continue to venture out and search for these creatures? It's possible that some people want the recognition that would come from discovery, but perhaps the real drive is the discovery itself. As a species, humans are curious. We want to explore and discover the world around us. And if these creatures exist in some hidden jungle or beneath the waves, we want to know.

This drive for discovery has helped us as a species advance beyond other animals. It's helped us explore the tops of mountains and the depths of the sea. It's helped us build complex rockets to explore the moon, the planets, and the stars. Curiosity keeps us from becoming stagnant. And so with cryptids, people wonder how much truth exists in those ancient stories and superstitions.

This book explores tales of some of the most well-known unexplained creatures. It turns to scientific approaches that have been applied to the search for these creatures, and examines the ways in which they have fascinated humanity since the first rumors of their existence.

PARANORMAL INVESTIGATING

It would seem that the idea of scientifically investigating paranormal activity wouldn't really work. If we could use traditional scientific methods of observations and experiments, the subjects we studied wouldn't really be paranormal. That doesn't stop paranormal investigators from trying to use scientific tools to prove that paranormal phenomena actually exist, though.

When people claim to have extrasensory perception (ESP), they will often undergo scientific tests to assess the validity of their claim. The testers often use tools like **Zener cards** to determine the individual's psychic ability. Ghost hunters use tools to try and establish patterns in ghost sightings by measuring environmental changes. Bigfoot hunters scour the woods looking for footprints and other evidence. By applying scientific principles to paranormal phenomena, researchers attempt to bring events and creatures out of the hidden corners and into the public eye.

This is a statue of a Yowie, an Australian creature similar to Bigfoot.

The History of Bigfoot

The giant apelike creature exists in many different folktales. These stories may all be slightly different, but the basic premise remains the same: an ape-man lives alone in the wilderness. Perhaps the fact that so many different civilizations have similar myths means that tales of the creature tap into a primal place in our brains, a longing for truth and discovery.

Bigfoot: Monster or Myth?

Whether or not Bigfoot actually exists depends on who you ask. There are those who believe without a doubt that he's real—they've seen him, heard him, smelled him while out camping or working in the forest. There are others who point to the lack of evidence despite years of searching, and claim that he is a figment of the imagination, born out of myths and stories and perpetuated by overeager people.

But maybe there is something to these myths. Bigfoot stories go back hundreds of years and were told by cultures that were completely separated from each other. They gave him different names and described him differently, but there are undeniable similarities to each story.

Hikers, campers, and everyday people have reported Bigfoot sightings all across the world. The first photographed "big foot," which gave the creature its name, was taken in the 1950s, and in 1967, the first filmed ape-man sighting occurred in the United States. However, these aren't just modern occurrences. Legends of such a creature permeated American and Canadian folklore a century before. Earlier still, some Bigfoot hunters claim that Viking Leif Eriksson witnessed Bigfoot—referred to as a "big hairy man"—while on an expedition in North America in 986 CE. In Nepal, mountain guides called Sherpas have stories of the Yeti, an ape-man living alone in the wilderness.

What Is Bigfoot Like?

According to legend, Bigfoot is a large, hairy **hominid** with a huge capacity for strength and excellent survival skills. Reports differ on his actual height, but most claim that he is taller than the average human, usually at least 6.5 feet (2 meters) tall. Stories describe him as having matted, dark fur that covers most or all of his body. He looks like an ape, usually with a large ridge over his eye sockets. This ridge is called the **sagittal crest**, and it is one of the defining facial characteristics of the gorilla.

There are differing reports regarding Bigfoot's diet, with some claiming that he is an herbivore that only eats plants found in the wilderness. People who believe Bigfoot is a vegetarian believe so because they compare him to a gorilla. Though gorillas are massive, they only eat plants and fruit. This opinion is not that popular, however. Most Bigfoot experts believe he is **omnivorous**, meaning that he'll eat both plants and animals, more like a chimpanzee. They believe he'll catch rabbits, hunt and kill deer, or even snatch fish out of streams or ponds. These experts claim that the forest habitats that Bigfoot

DID TEDDY ROOSEVELT BELIEVE IN BIGFOOT?

Teddy Roosevelt is known for many things. He was the twenty-sixth president of the United States, an avid hunter, and the ultimate outdoorsman. He wasn't superstitious, but he did seem to believe a story once told to him by an old hunting partner named Bauman. He related the tale in his book *The Wilderness Hunter*.

President Roosevelt was an enthusiastic outdoorsman.

As the story went, when Bauman was younger, he was out trapping and hunting with a partner. One night, they were attacked in their campsite but drove away what they thought was a bear. Once the sun came up, they examined the tracks and realized that the beast had walked on two legs and had human-like prints. Spooked, they continued their work.

When Bauman went to check beaver traps, he left his partner alone. Returning to camp later, he found his partner dead, bitten several times by some unknown creature and with a broken neck. The tracks around the corpse matched the large bipedal tracks they had found the night before. Bauman rode off as fast as he could, frightened and worried that the beast might soon be back.

is usually sighted near don't have the lush and edible plant life that sustains gorillas. Therefore, to survive in the Pacific Northwest, where many of the US sightings take place, Bigfoot would have to hunt game.

Survival means more than finding food, though. Like all animals, Bigfoot would need to find shelter to survive rainy nights and cold winters. Several researchers have found nests that seem to be likely Bigfoot bedding. If these experts are correct, Bigfoot collects leaves and grasses to create a space to lie down for a short time, then will get up and move on.

Some cryptozoologists believe that Bigfoot takes shelter in caves. These would be attractive places for Bigfoot to live. After all, they're protected, have a relatively consistent temperature, and would keep the creature away from predators and humans looking to find him. However, many experts believe that Bigfoot is nomadic. They say that staying in a single place for too long would exhaust the food source, and Bigfoot would then be forced to venture further out.

The Search for Bigfoot

No one knows who first discovered Bigfoot because there have been so many sightings around the world. In the Pacific Northwest region of the United States, he is usually referred to as Bigfoot or Sasquatch. In the Southeastern region of the United States, near Florida and Louisiana, they call him "Skunk Ape." In the Himalayan Mountains, he is the Yeti, living in the snowy mountains. When the British led an expedition to explore Mount Everest, they called the Yeti the "Abominable Snowman." In Australia, he is called a Yowie and has roots in aboriginal oral histories.

While each of these creatures is slightly different, they all share some telling characteristics. Each are apelike and larger than the average person. They are all covered in hair, are very strong, and prefer to remain hidden.

Because so many different people from so many different cultures have similar descriptions of the creature, some are convinced that Bigfoot must be real. Because these sightings are all independent and have their roots in completely different cultural histories, Bigfoot believers claim that there must be some truth behind those stories, and they set out to find physical proof to back up the myths. Bigfoot hunters set up cameras, study possible nests, and set bait to try to lure Bigfoot out into the open.

Skeptics not only point to the lack of physical proof of Bigfoot but claim that a large breeding population would be

GIVING THE SKEPTICS SOME CREDIT

As long as there have been storytellers, there have been skeptics. For these people, the stories told around campfires have no basis in fact and shouldn't be seen as reality in any way. They usually want people to understand what these tales actually are: old stories that have outlived their usefulness as warnings and should be treated as fictional tales.

Skeptics play an important role in the search for cryptids. By holding claims of evidence to a scientifically rigorous process, they ensure that people are not able to commit countless **hoaxes** and reap financial rewards associated with the discoveries. By going into every encounter with doubt, they resist being swayed by nonscientific evidence, and help the public remain grounded in their beliefs.

Bigfoot may have a similar physiology to large, known apes like this mountain gorilla.

needed to sustain the species. In order for a species to remain **viable,** a certain number of male and female members of the species must be able to produce offspring. By all accounts, Bigfoot is a solitary creature and is rarely seen in the company of others like him. Skeptics claim that if viable Bigfoot populations actually existed, finding evidence wouldn't be as difficult because there would just be more of them out there, and the chances of a provable encounter would be higher.

Neither side can offer anything definitive or completely convincing, so the debate continues. Interest in finding Bigfoot remains as high as ever, and there are a few reasons this might be. Bigfoot seems like a realistic creature in that he acts and lives much in the way we would expect a woodland creature to act. Sustained interest might also have something to do with our similarities with the creature. After all, people are fascinated with the mannerisms and behaviors of other great apes, like gorillas and chimpanzees, due to their commonalities with human beings. Perhaps finding Bigfoot is a way to examine our own social and survival instincts by comparing them with another primate that exists in our world. While concrete evidence hasn't been confirmed, it isn't a stretch to believe that Bigfoot can exist, somewhere in the wild.

BIGFOOT IN A FREEZER

Bigfoot has been spotted by many people across many cultures, but in June 2008, two men claimed to have found him. Friends Matt Whitton and Rick Dyer said they had found the body of Bigfoot while hiking in the woods in Georgia. They were able to drag it inside and keep it in a freezer. After posting videos on YouTube, they called several press conferences with local Sasquatch-searching shows and local television stations, and had researchers run tests. However, when the test results came back, they proved what most people thought: that the Bigfoot in the freezer was a fake. In reality, Whitton and Dyer had bought a rubber ape costume and stuffed it with opossum guts.

After being confronted about the hoax, Whitton and Dyer reportedly admitted to perpetrating it, but their reasons for doing so were never well established. Steve Kulls, a Bigfoot enthusiast, reported that he suspected the two were financially motivated and that they had requested a sum of money up front for their story. The hoax only lasted a few days before being disproven.

Perhaps the most famous image of Bigfoot is a still from the Patterson-Gimlin film. Here, the creature looks over its shoulder into the camera.

CHAPTER TWO

Finding Bigfoot

In October 1967, Roger Patterson and his friend Bob Gimlin were riding horses through a forest in Northern California when suddenly, a creature appeared in the distance. The horses reared up, but Patterson, a former rodeo rider, was able to steady his horse enough to grab his video camera and film the encounter. The resulting footage captured an apelike creature walking through the woods. After about five seconds of walking away from the camera, the creature turned around and looked directly at the person filming. The creature then continued its jaunt into the forest, disappearing quickly from view. It is a grainy representation, but the two men were convinced they had found Bigfoot.

Since then, there have been many believers and nonbelievers in the Bigfoot myth. Some people have dedicated their entire lives to the search for the creature, believing he is out there. Some have spent thousands of dollars on equipment to analyze evidence, fund expeditions into the wilderness, and purchase cameras to watch the woods for Bigfoot passing by. Others might not have believed in Bigfoot until they had their own chance encounter, maybe seeing something hairy rustling in the bushes near their tents or finding strange footprints while hiking. But how can these believers convince others that Bigfoot actually exists?

Standard Methods

While the larger scientific community has more or less decided that Bigfoot is the stuff of imagination and hoaxes, cryptozoologists try to use scientific methods to prove that their beliefs have merit. Usually, this is done through hard evidence. Many would think that photographs of the animal would count as evidence, but the public has been fooled too many times before to take a photograph at face value, especially when it comes to high-profile cryptids like Bigfoot. There is a long history of people trying to use Bigfoot sightings as a way to either increase their own personal fame or to play jokes on the people around them. Many crytozoologists turn to a different kind of camera, one that can capture moving images, to try to reveal Bigfoot's true nature.

In addition to film, older, less intensive methods of hunting Bigfoot remain. Most amateur hunters wander the woods looking for tracks, bedding, and other signs that Bigfoot has been in an area. If they see signs, they may hang around, waiting to see if he'll return. But because Bigfoot is notoriously shy, it has proven difficult to catch glimpses of him with human-controlled equipment.

Tools for Hunting

One of the most important tools for hunting Bigfoot is a motion-sensitive camera called a trail camera, or "trail cam" for short. Usually used to track endangered or nocturnal animals, trail cameras are attached to trees and left unattended for days—or even months—at a time. If Bigfoot wandered by, one of these cameras could snap a photo. These trail cameras also have the advantage of operating independently of any human-controlled input. A hunter could purchase hundreds of cameras and strategically place them, effectively watching a much larger area than would otherwise be possible.

Some Bigfoot believers think that a trail cam has already captured an image of Bigfoot. In 2007, one such camera in Pennsylvania took a photo of a hairy animal lumbering through the forest. While the photo didn't show anything very clearly, it did seem to show an animal with long, apelike arms. The creature also seemed to be walking on its knuckles, lending further evidence to those who want to believe in Bigfoot. Skeptics dismiss the photograph as inconclusive. They say that the animal is likely just a **mangy**, thin bear that was caught in an awkward pose.

Another tool in the Bigfoot hunter's arsenal is an infrared camera. This camera, also called a thermal imaging camera or a thermographic camera, forms an image by detecting infrared radiation. Most commonly, people think of these cameras as "heat-seeking" cameras. Objects and animals that emit

Infrared cameras allow people to see objects that emit heat, like this cat running across a field.

heat show up in various colors against contrasting colored backgrounds. Because Bigfoot is a mammal, these thermal imaging techniques would help hunters spot him against the cold rocks and trees.

Thermal imaging cameras work very well for hunting Bigfoot because the ambient light levels do not matter. This means that they work in darkness as well as in daylight. With these special cameras, hunters can watch for Bigfoot's movements without disturbing him.

THE SKOOKUM CAST

While there are many plaster casts of Bigfoot's footprints (*right*), there are also suggestions that Bigfoot beds down and leaves full and partial body imprints on the ground. One of these imprints is referred to as the Skookum Cast.

In 2000, Bigfoot researchers found evidence of a partial body imprint in some roadside mud. They created a cast and began to study the way the body had lain in the mud. While the researchers claim that it had all the telltale signs of an apelike creature, a more through analysis shows that

This man compares his foot to that of a cast of "Bigfoot's."

it's most likely the imprint of an elk, as evidenced by the presence of elk hair and imprints of an elk's legs. The mistake is understandable, however. The researchers were in the wilderness looking for signs of Bigfoot. They should have exercised restraint and looked for more facts before jumping to conclusions.

The Patterson-Gimlin Film

Since its introduction in 1967, the Patterson-Gimlin film has been examined and reexamined countless times. Those who do not believe the footage claim it is merely a person in a monkey suit and mask, purposely shot in a way that makes it difficult to see how the figure moves. They argue that the walk of the creature is very much like the walk of a human, including the way that the arms swing and how the knees and ankles bend around the terrain. Skeptics also point to the fact that Gimlin and Patterson, when interviewed separately, gave different versions of the story. They didn't agree on the creature's size, nor were they consistent in detailing how the horses they were riding reacted upon seeing the creature. While these details might be minor, in an event like a Bigfoot sighting, they are magnified.

Those who believe the video shows real evidence cite the fact that after shooting, Roger Patterson immediately had all of the film developed and tried to show everyone right away. He even tried to get a tracking dog to attempt to hunt down the creature that day. The sense of urgency, some claim, shows that he was not trying to perpetuate a hoax, but instead to inform people about what he saw. Some also cite the fact that if Patterson and Gimlin were motivated to create a hoax, they simply would have done a better job at it. They say that they would have used a more convincing costume, or that they would have planned out exactly what they were going to say so that they could avoid any inconsistencies in their stories.

It's difficult to say whether or not the film is a hoax, and indeed people have been arguing about it since the film was published. Roger Patterson maintained that the video was real up to his dying day in 1972. Bob Gimlin, on the other hand, declined to talk about the film for most of his life, only recently attending Bigfoot conferences. It isn't likely that one side will convince the other of the video's authenticity, so the debate will continue for a long time.

Video Evidence Perpetuates the Myth

Video remains a powerful tool to convince people something exists. In the past few years, there has been renewed interest in providing video evidence of Bigfoot and other cryptids. Some cable television channels like the History Channel and Animal Planet have begun airing specials and even creating season-long television shows that detail several Bigfoot hunters and their endeavors to track and locate the creature.

These television shows try to cultivate interest in hunting for the creature as well as introduce scientific evidence to compliment any videos that they find. One such Bigfoot-related documentary on the National Geographic Channel, *Bigfoot: The New Evidence*, took host Mark Evans on a search around the world. Rather than relying solely on video documentation and eyewitness reports, he went to individual cities and villages reporting to have actual Yeti and Bigfoot artifacts. Evans traveled around the world collecting samples of these artifacts—skin tissue, fur, and even a whole Bigfoot hand—and then had them tested at a laboratory. The results, for some, were surprising. All of the samples, even the seemingly most obscure, were confirmed to come from different types of bears. Still, villagers and eyewitnesses continue to be fascinated by the Bigfoot myth, convinced that the creature is very real.

Bigfoot researchers want the public interested in their work for many reasons. Most importantly, if there's more interest, search expeditions will be better funded with more sophisticated equipment and more people doing the hunting.

People use cameras to watch the forest for signs of Bigfoot. This artist's rendition shows what a trail cam might see.

The Trouble with TV

TV shows also deal with many problems facing video-only evidence of Bigfoot. **False positives** happen often, especially with people who are hopeful to find evidence. That is why there's a big emphasis on finding corroborating evidence to support any footage. Video evidence alone is easy to dismiss as a hoax or as a misidentified animal.

Some amateur Bigfoot hunters use cameras like this to try to find the ape-man.

The problem with video evidence—especially when it is funded by a television or movie studio—is that researchers may feel pressured to "jazz up" their findings or try to make their hunts more dramatic. Misidentified animals become important for maintaining ratings. Several television shows have faced criticism from Bigfoot researchers—even those that appeared on the show. Many claim the television networks use deceptive editing to create tension and even imply that several disproven sightings were actually possible authentic sightings. The entertainment factor with hunting for Bigfoot is a real danger to the scientific mindset that most researchers strive for. They take their hunting very seriously and fear that using their processes for entertainment value cheapens the real work they are trying to do.

JOHN GREEN: PROMINENT INVESTIGATOR

John Green is considered by some to be the godfather of Bigfoot research. He began investigating Bigfoot sightings and tracks in 1957 and created a career devoted to determining the existence of the creature. Green also wrote several books on Sasquatch, including the remarkably influential *Sasquatch: The Apes Among Us.*

As he worked, Green became the go-to expert on validating or dismissing Bigfoot sightings and tracks. He investigated prominent reports, including the famous Patterson-Gimlin film, which he seemed to believe was an authentic video. Through all of his research, he compiled an enormous database of more than three thousand Bigfoot reports. Green was an influential figure in Bigfoot studies until his death on May 28, 2016, and he remains influential to this day.

Many people believe the
Loch Ness Monster looks
like a plesiosaur.

CHAPTER THREE

The Origins of Nessie

L ike Bigfoot, the legend of the Loch Ness Monster has fascinated believers and nonbelievers for decades. Affectionately known as Nessie, this ancient sea creature is said to lurk in the tranquil waters of Loch Ness, near Inverness, Scotland. Stories of sea monsters have permeated many cultures for centuries, but only since the first photograph of the Loch Ness Monster arrived in 1933 did many start to believe, and the modern myth was born.

Water Creatures

Water monsters are popular subjects for stories and myths. Usually such tales are set on the ocean, where vast unexplored and unmonitored areas make the perfect places for strange and supernatural encounters.

For eons, people have wondered what might lie in the oceans, so dark and deep. Ancient sailors voyaged out to sea, risking their safety while working to connect trade routes, provide security, and explore the world. When they returned home, they told of the wild things they had seen. They spun tales of epic sea monsters like the kraken, with its enormous ship-smashing arms, and sea serpents that could pluck sailors off the decks of their ship, dooming men to watery graves.

Because sailing was so difficult and dangerous, people believed the tales, thinking such stories could explain why so many ships were lost on the waters. All of these stories were told and retold, creating a rich and intricate sea-monster culture.

The legend of the Loch Ness Monster follows a tradition of water creatures stretching back centuries. In Celtic folklore, water creatures have resided in lakes and rivers. The Scottish kelpie, a water spirit, lures children into lochs and drags them down to the bottom, killing them. The Irish, Scottish, and Icelandic selkie, a seal that can turn into a human, stuns people with his or her beauty and has inspired many stories. These tales play an important role in culture. They not only act as warnings against dangerous locations and activities, but they offer a sense of community in their retellings. Sharing stories with neighbors and friends helps build a community's identity, and the Loch Ness Monster has helped to frame the identity of one Scottish town. It's a pretty unique identity to have a famous sea serpent swimming around!

Sailors feared the mythical kraken, which was said to be able to sink even the largest ships.

Nessie

Tales of the Loch Ness Monster are confined to a single area, the waters of Loch Ness. Surrounded by cliffs, woods, and even a ruined castle, this area seems a rather picturesque place for such a creature to live.

Loch Ness is large and deep, with a surface area of about 22 miles (35 kilometers) and an average depth of about 430 feet (131 m), although in certain areas, the lake gets as deep as 744 feet (227 m). The estimated total water in Loch Ness is 1.8 cubic miles (7.5 cubic kilometers). However, it is not even one of the larger lakes in the world! For comparison, the smallest North American great lake (by surface area) is Lake Ontario, which has a square footage of over 7,000 square miles (18,129 square kilometers). Lake Ontario has 292 cubic miles (1,217 cubic km) of water in it!

In theory, it should be fairly easy to find a large animal living in a lake that size. However, Loch Ness remains quite mysterious because the water is very murky with lots of soil mixed in. The murkiness makes it difficult to see anything in the water—and this may be why the tale of the Loch Ness Monster persists.

What Is Nessie Like?

Descriptions of the Loch Ness Monster sometimes characterize the beast as some kind of living dinosaur, a descendant of an ancient species that lives beneath the waves. In popular culture, the plesiosaur is a useful stand-in for the Loch Ness Monster. There isn't a unified description of what the creature looks like, but common sightings describe a large reptile with a long neck and a humped back that rises out of the water when it surfaces.

Other Nessie hunters don't think of the monster as an ancient dinosaur, but instead see it as some sort of sea serpent or enormous eel. They doubt that the Loch Ness Monster can get out of the water and walk around but think it stays below the waves much of the time.

Finding Nessie

As with Bigfoot, sightings of the Loch Ness Monster are rooted in ancient stories. The first mention of a monster appearing near Loch Ness was recorded sometime in the sixth century CE as part of the *Life of Saint Columba*. While there isn't a physical description of the creature in the text, it is the first recorded monster sighting around Loch Ness. The description of the Loch Ness Monster makes the beast sound more like a standard monster. In the text, Saint Columba, a respected saint in the Roman Catholic tradition, comes across a young man who had been "savagely bitten by a water beast" with a "gaping mouth." Columba commanded the monster to leave, and it swam away. The description of the beast is not specific, but nonetheless, this record spurred curiosity about a monster near a loch in Scotland.

For generations after, strange events were noted around Loch Ness, perpetuating the myth. In the 1500s, a local man named Duncan Campbell saw a large creature on the shore. He described it as a "terrible beast." In 1879, children reported seeing a long-necked creature on the north shore of the loch. A few decades later, a husband and wife were near Loch Ness when they saw a large beast cross the street in front of their car. The man said that the beast lumbered toward the water and tore up the trees and grass around the road. Not long after, a motorcyclist saw a similar-looking beast cross the road. He jumped off his bike and went to check it out. He only caught up in time to see something dark slip below the waves. These sightings kicked off a hunt for the creature, and eventually, new research sprang to life.

The Modern Nessie

In the 1930s, having photographic evidence of something was very important. Photography had begun about one hundred years earlier, but in the 1930s, it was still in its early stages. Many people living during that time thought a photo couldn't be altered. To them, this meant a photograph lent legitimacy to any claim. The first reported image of something lurking in the waters was published in the *Inverness Courier* on November 12, 1933. Hugh Gray, a resident of the area, had taken the photo, but it was difficult to discern. It could've been a surfacing fish or a log. Whatever it was, it seemed to be moving when the image was snapped. However, perceptions changed when another photo of the Loch Ness Monster arose in 1934.

Marmaduke Wetherell (*center*) inspects evidence of the Loch Ness Monster.

The photographer of this image was R.K. Wilson, a surgeon from London. He had heard stories about people seeing a large beast around and in the loch, so he decided to investigate. While there, he snapped the photo that would dazzle the world and convince many that the Loch Ness Monster was not just imagination.

In 1934, the UK-based *Daily Mail* printed the now-famous image, called the *Surgeon's Photograph*. This photo was grainy but featured a dinosaur-like creature surfacing the loch. Many people used it to confirm their suspicions. Beyond providing evidence for people who believed in the mythical creature, the photograph caused the world to catch "Nessie fever," and even those who had never heard of the Loch Ness Monster were able to learn about the beast.

Suddenly, everyone had an opinion on Nessie. Some people maintained that she was lurking in the water, while most chalked all the sightings up to overactive imaginations, driftwood, and a series of cleverly designed hoaxes. So many people wanted some sort of definitive proof that roads were built up around the loch, providing access to places that were once more remote.

Today, sightings of the monster have leveled off some, but people continue to report seeing Nessie every year. Many think that because so many previous sightings were confirmed as hoaxes, the enthusiasm to keep scouring the lake has waned. That hasn't stopped some individuals, though. Nessie hunters continue to take boats onto the loch and search for signs of the elusive creature. And as technology advances, hunters use new equipment to search. Sometimes, searchers don't even have to be in Scotland to hunt for Nessie! In 2014, numerous people reported that a satellite image on Apple Maps showed the Loch Ness Monster. The image is blurry, but it appears to be a large, fish-like creature with several fins and an enormous head. Skeptics were quick to point out that it might be the wake of a boat, or a seal, or even just a glitch in the mapping cameras. But the recency of this sighting shows that people remain interested in finding the Loch Ness Monster to this day.

Loch Ness itself has become so associated with the monster that Nessie-themed gift shops, toys, jewelry, and tours are offered each year by local visitor centers.

MARMADUKE WETHERELL

Marmaduke Wetherell plays an interesting and strange role in the legend of the Loch Ness Monster. Wetherell was a big-game hunter who was tasked by the *Daily Mail* in 1933 to find evidence of the creature after multiple eyewitness reports were filed. After only a few days of searching, he announced that he had found large footprints from a four-toed animal that he estimated to be at least 20 feet (6 m) long!

After a few weeks of excitement around the loch, things took a turn. Museum zoologists researched the plaster casts that Wetherell had made and announced that the tracks were identical, and from a hippo—more specifically, a hippo-leg umbrella stand.

Wetherell would also be remembered as part of the team that staged the *Surgeon's Photograph* in 1934.

THE SURGEON'S PHOTOGRAPH

Even though the famous photo amplified the craze to find the Loch Ness Monster, most people agree that it was part of an elaborate hoax to fool the public. While the photo initially seems impressive, the *Daily Mail* originally cropped the photo to make the creature/object appear larger than it actually was. By offering some perspective, the object seems to be much smaller—maybe only 2 or 3 feet (0.6 or 0.9 m) long—hardly the enormous monster that people expected to find.

A man named Christian Spurling also came forward in 1994 to confess that he helped build the elaborate model to perpetuate the hoax. He told reporters that he fashioned a toy submarine to have a head that looked like a sea serpent, and that the model was used to stage the famous photograph.

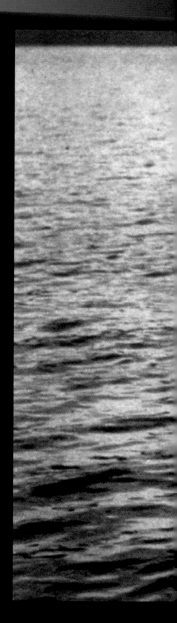

The famous *Surgeon's Photograph* allegedly shows a long neck and head emerging from Loch Ness.

Lachlan Stuart's photograph shows three small humps rising out of the water, which many thought belonged to Nessie.

CHAPTER FOUR

Investigating the Loch Ness Monster

L ike with Bigfoot, the easiest method of searching for the Loch Ness Monster is to go out onto the loch or by the shoreline and look for it. It's possible that by gazing at the water, you'll be able to see the monster poke its head above the waves or make a large splash somewhere in the distance. For years, this was the primary method of searching for the Loch Ness Monster—and it produced some interesting photos. However, because science requires that a method be replicable and adhere to experimental guidelines, "going out and looking at the loch" is not the most scientific way to hunt for the ancient cryptid.

Methods to Find Nessie

The general public tends to believe videos more than still photographs. There's something about seeing the way something moves that helps lend believability to the experience. Videos also seem harder and more expensive to fake. This is why many Nessie hunters bring video cameras to try to catch a glimpse of the beast. Besides the benefit of being able to show what you've seen to others, having multiple video cameras can give hunters a wider range of what they can see.

Several videos claiming to feature the Loch Ness Monster have surfaced in the past few years. None of them offer a clear look at the creature, though, except for those that have been debunked as hoaxes. Possible credible videos of Nessie tend to focus more on dark shapes emerging from the water for a few seconds and then submerging again, creating a large whirlpool that leaves people marveling at the size of the creature. With this kind of footage, some remain hopeful that it will only be a matter of time before video evidence shows a clear image of Nessie.

LACHLAN STUART'S PHOTOGRAPH

In 1951, a man named Lachlan Stuart submitted a photograph to newspapers that supposedly showed the Loch Ness Monster rising from the water. The hazy photograph shows three small humps sticking out of the water. The three humps lined up to show that the monster supposedly slithered through the water like a snake.

The hoax didn't last long, though. In the 1970s, a researcher went to the exact spot that the photograph was taken and noticed that the creature would have been in incredibly shallow water. After suspicions were raised, a local author named Richard Frere revealed that Stuart told him he merely covered three bales of hay with a tarp and then snapped the photograph. The Stuart photograph is just one more example of someone trying to find fame by staging photos.

Sonar Searching

Video cameras can only see what peeks out from under the surface, though, and Nessie famously loves to stay underneath the water. That's why, in the 1950s, researchers started using sonar to hunt for the creature. Sonar is an invaluable tool because it doesn't rely on visibility. Instead, it sends out a pulse of sound and then listens for the echo. By measuring how the sound returns, people can use sonar to do all sorts of things. They can map the ocean floor, look for submarines, and track marine life. So it's only natural that Nessie hunters would use sonar to try to prove her existence.

While there have been many sonar studies, very few actually show any possible monster findings. The most widespread effort happened in the late 1960s, when hunters set up a sonar reader on one side of the loch and pointed it over the rest of the water. They then tested for two weeks, capturing any movements and recording the expected size, speed, and any other patterns. When the experiment finished, they were left with mixed results. Most of the readings could be explained

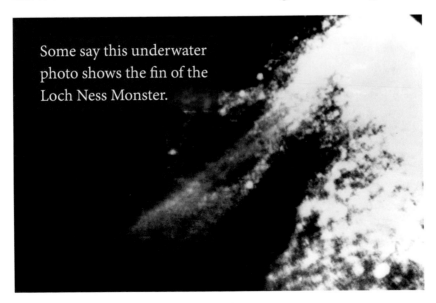

Some say this underwater photo shows the fin of the Loch Ness Monster.

as moving shoals of fish or large, inanimate objects. However, there was one reading that showed an object making a dive at a speed of about 6 miles per hour (10 kmh).

ROBERT RINES

Robert H. Rines was a renowned American lawyer and inventor who devoted much of his life to searching for the Loch Ness Monster. While visiting Scotland in 1972, he and his wife saw a strange grey hump emerge from the water. They stared at it for ten minutes until

Dr. Robert Rines (*left*) adjusts his Nessie-hunting equipment.

it dove back down into the depths. Convinced that he had seen the Loch Ness Monster, Rines decided that he would try his hardest to find scientific proof that the monster existed.

Rines not only conducted countless expeditions to try to find the monster, but he also created and patented new technology that would help him hunt. This included improvements to sonar equipment and a scent specifically concocted to attract Nessie. As time went by, Rines worried that the monster may have died while he was searching for it; he began to shift away from hunting and back toward education and encouraging students to invent new things. He died in November 2009, still believing that he had seen the fabled creature.

This illustration shows how sonar works.

While many believed that these readings showed evidence of the Loch Ness Monster, the research institute urged caution. After reading the reports, Colin Muir, a lecturer from St. Andrews University, said that a 6-mile-per-hour (10 kmh) dive isn't really all that fast, and noted that "salmon, for instance, dive at eight miles an hour [13 kmh] when they are being chased." However, neither independent researchers nor those who completed the experiment could say definitively what the diving object actually was. In absence of an explanation, those who believe that the Loch Ness Monster is out there see these readings as support for their viewpoint. Skeptics dismiss these sonar results by explaining that the blip on the machine is a grouping of fish, a seal, or a clump of algae.

But sonar readings aren't used by themselves. Often, researchers will use sonar to better hone their other experiments. Sometimes, smaller sonar readers are attached to boats, and researchers travel around the loch taking readings. This way, they can track movements with greater accuracy and follow any interesting readings. Sometimes, researchers will drop a waterproof camera with powerful floodlights over the side of the boat if their sonars detect anything interesting in the depths. It's difficult to get good pictures beneath the waves because the water is so murky.

In one of these studies, an underwater camera snapped a photo of an object some say is the flipper of the Loch Ness Monster. If you look at the photo, you can see a light object against a dark background. The light object has some stark edges that seem to have the rounded edges of a flipper. The stark contrast of the dark background helps the flipper stand out. However, there are skeptics who say the photo was altered, that the background was purposely shaded to highlight the contrast, and if the photo wasn't doctored, it would look much more like a rock or a piece of driftwood against the lakebed.

So, without any concrete evidence, the hunt for Nessie continues. However, with the improvement of technology, more opportunities to investigate sightings will arise. Who knows? We may find Nessie in Loch Ness's depths one day after all.

CHAMPY: A DISTANT RELATIVE?

Nessie is not the only well-known lake monster. There might be one living in North America! Lake Champlain, on the border of Vermont and New York, is rumored to harbor a Nessie-like creature that locals refer to as "Champ" or "Champy." Lake Champlain is a much larger lake than Loch Ness, so there's much more space for a monster to hide.

Most sightings claim that Champy is a large plesiosaur-like creature, similar to reports of the Loch Ness Monster—though it's not clear if the sightings took on those characteristics after reports of Nessie made their way to the United States. It's possible that earlier sightings of Champy were more serpent-like, fitting in with the more traditional sea monster myths.

The legend of Champy emerged in earnest in the mid 1800s when sightings of a "large black beast" began to appear. Some reports were fairly generic, but others were remarkably specific, with references to a star on the forehead of the creature and eyes "the color of a peeled onion." The reports were so intriguing and so widespread that famed circus promoter P.T. Barnum offered $50,000 in 1873 to anyone who could capture and skin Champy to prove its existence. In today's terms, that would be an almost $1 million reward! This offer sparked a great search, but no evidence of Champy was sufficient to collect.

Champy still gets sighted today, but at a far lower frequency and with far less fanfare. Sightings seem to come in waves, with a lot of reports clustering together. So far, no one has offered convincing evidence that Champy exists, but many are still hopeful. Tourism around Lake Champlain partially relies on the fame that Champy brings the region, so there are reasons for perpetuating the myth and allowing people to come and hunt for the creature.

With large areas of forest still unexplored and unmonitored, it's possible that Bigfoot lurks in the wilderness.

What Difference Does It Make?

If you think about it, it seems fairly inconsequential if the Loch Ness Monster and Bigfoot actually exist in nature. After all, there are countless unidentified species that exist in the far reaches of the forest or in the oceans. What does it matter if there really is a great ape that wanders around the Pacific Northwest or an ancient dinosaur relative living at the bottom of a Scottish loch? Why should anyone care about these things?

Besides the overall pursuit of knowledge and discovery that goes along with searching for any new species, there is the satisfaction of knowing the answer to a centuries-old mystery. Wouldn't it be cool to know if all those people who claimed to see Nessie walk across the road and descend into the cold murky water actually saw it? Wouldn't it be interesting to discover that the people who have spent their lives hunting for an elusive ape creature were right all along? Or is it better to live with the mystery? After all, as soon as science can explain a cryptid, the magic will disappear into cold factuality.

Part of Nessie and Bigfoot's lasting power comes from the intricate and varied stories that people tell about them. Bigfoot is simultaneously an ape, a humanoid creature, a gentle soul, and a terrifying beast that can rip a person limb from limb. Because he

The Loch Ness Monster appears throughout popular culture. This image is from the 2007 movie *The Water Horse: Legend of the Deep*.

can be all things to all people, Bigfoot is an enduring character—and as people, we love interesting characters.

So while the science is still out on these two creatures, we may ask ourselves what it would mean for us to discover the truth. Science does an excellent job explaining the world around us, but it cannot provide proof that something cannot exist. So while it may be frustrating to those people who do not believe in these cryptids, there will always be those individuals who "know" Bigfoot and Nessie are out there—we just need to find them.

Future Investigations

Technology is constantly changing and evolving. With each technological advancement also come new strategies and tools for hunting cryptids. Clearer photos, more convincing videos, more efficient planning and searching—all of these advances can help give investigators the edge they've been looking for in tracking down evidence of these elusive, legendary creatures.

Bigfoot researchers are also starting to use **drones**. Jeff Meldrum, an Idaho State University professor, recently launched a search for Bigfoot in the Cascade Mountain Range using drones equipped with thermal imaging equipment. These drones can cover a greater area and can get a better viewpoint of a larger area. The thermal imaging is important because the forest is thick and visibility over a long range is low. Even though most of the professor's colleagues are skeptical and think that the search for Bigfoot is a waste of resources, Bigfoot hunters are hopeful that these newly equipped drones will help find convincing evidence of the creature's existence.

Urquhart Castle overlooks
Loch Ness, Scotland.

Recently, satellite imaging has emerged as a new, more affordable tool than it has been in the past. By analyzing high-quality maps, researchers can chart probable Bigfoot habitats, or even catch a glimpse of one lying down and taking a nap. Unfortunately, a photo probably won't convince the general public, but by analyzing patterns of movement, researchers can better chart their searches.

On a 2003 expedition looking for the Loch Ness Monster, satellite tracking was used, along with sonar readings, to get a better idea of how large objects are moving in the loch and what they might actually be. The BBC sponsored this search, which involved six hundred separate sonar beams and satellite navigation to make sure that nothing was missed. The search team hoped that they could find some kind of **anomaly** in the data that might indicate the possibility of a large creature in the loch. After running all the tests, they were disappointed not to find any signs of a large living animal. According to their research, Nessie is a myth that continues to live on because people want it to.

Because people want to believe in cryptids and other strange phenomena, no amount of scientific experimentation is going to change some people's minds about a creature's existence. Even after the 2003 sonar study that effectively proved there was no monster living in Loch Ness, people continue to report sightings of a monster's head poking out of the water. The desire to believe in these sorts of things is very powerful.

What Do You Think?

People have been trying for years to find hard scientific evidence of Bigfoot, the Loch Ness Monster, and other cryptids. So far, they haven't been able to come up with anything that convinces skeptics or the general public. Most people believe Bigfoot is a series of misidentified animals or repeated cases of an overactive imagination. After the sonar studies of Loch Ness, many people resigned to the idea that maybe the monster that lived in the loch was an illusion and a fun story that they could tell their friends.

But there are many people out there who really do believe in these creatures. They think it's just a matter of time before they're proven right, and the photographs that they've seen or taken or the personal encounters with cryptids that they've had are real and not something made up. Ultimately, the decision to believe or not lies with you.

Do paranormal creatures exist?

BELIEF, DISBELIEF, AND HUMAN NATURE

It's interesting to see how universal some of these myths are. So many different cultures around the world have developed similar myths and stories, and while some are very unique to their time and place, others have a sense of similarity. Why do you think that is? How is it that old stories of Bigfoot can be found all across the world?

It's possible that these stories are created someplace deep in the human mind, and that the stories reflect something innately human about the storytellers. Believing and remembering these stories may have helped with our survival when times were tough. Stories that warned of danger in the dark forest or in the depths of the water may have been enough to keep others away from the real dangers of getting lost in the forest or drowning in water that seemed calm. Having a scary monster lurking nearby would be a useful tool to discourage risky behavior!

Today similar methods are applied at campsites and other forested areas to warn the public of possible wildlife encounters. Signs, such as Bigfoot Crossing (*right*), appear as a sort of tongue-in-cheek notice. However, they also seek to educate others of possible dangers in the area, and engage the imagination by stating, quite clearly, that Bigfoot may be among them. ⁃

A "Bigfoot Crossing" sign warns hikers to be cautious of all wildlife in the area.

BIG FOOT XING

DUE TO SIGHTINGS IN THE AREA OF A CREATURE RESEMBLING "BIG FOOT" THIS SIGN HAS BEEN POSTED FOR YOUR SAFETY

GLOSSARY

anomaly Not adhering to what is normal or expected. An outlier or an abnormality.

cryptid A creature that cannot yet be proven or disproven through science.

cryptozoologist A researcher that specializes in the study of cryptids.

debunk To prove to be false. Usually happens when a paranormal claim is proven to be impossible through scientific evidence or confession.

drone A small, remote-controlled robot that can fly. It often has a camera attached.

false positive A test result that comes back positive but is actually proven negative after completing other tests.

hoax A prank or a trick. It can be done for monetary gain or just for fun.

hominid Any primate that walks on two legs. This includes humans as well as gorillas, chimpanzees, and orangutans.

mangy Diseased and scabbed over. In mammals, this often means having patchy hair.

omnivorous An animal that eats both plants and other animals to survive.

sagittal crest A bony ridge on the top of the skull.

skeptic A person who has a questioning attitude and desires scientific evidence before believing a claim.

viable Capable of surviving for the long-term. In the case of species, it means having enough of a population to produce offspring.

Zener cards A set of cards with five different symbols. It is used to test ESP.

FURTHER INFORMATION

Books

Brockenbrough, Martha. *Finding Bigfoot: Everything You Need to Know*. New York: Feiwel and Friends, 2013.

Green, John. *Sasquatch: The Apes Among Us*. Saanichton, British Columbia: Hancock House, 1978.

Krensky, Stephen. *Bigfoot*. Minneapolis, MN: Lerner Publications, 2007.

Sievert, Terri. *The Unsolved Mystery of the Loch Ness Monster*. Unexplained Mysteries. North Mankato, MN: Capstone, 2013.

Websites

The Bigfoot Field Researchers Organization
http://www.bfro.net

The Bigfoot Field Researchers Organization is a society dedicated to finding scientific evidence of Bigfoot. This site exists to keep people updated on sightings and other news.

Legend of Nessie: the Ultimate Loch Ness Monster Site
http://www.nessie.co.uk

Calling itself "the ultimate and official Loch Ness Monster site," this website offers visitors historical listings of sightings, evidence, and even a live webcam of the loch.

The Museum of Hoaxes

http://hoaxes.org

The Museum of Hoaxes website details the many hoaxes that exist in our world.

Videos

MonsterQuest

https://www.youtube.com/watch?v=zPIj4W4kUB0

This episode of the History Channel show details the modern hunt for Bigfoot.

Patterson-Gimlin Film

https://www.youtube.com/watch?v=IJjUt2sXo5o

This is the famous Bigfoot-encounter film that sparked thousands of debates about the creature's existence.

BIBLIOGRAPHY

Adamnan, and Wentworth Huyshe. *The Life of Saint Columba.* London, UK: Routledge, 1905.

"BBC 'proves' Nessie Does Not Exist." BBC News. July 27, 2003. http://news.bbc.co.uk/2/hi/science/nature/3096839.stm.

"Bigfoot Caught on Tape (Patterson Footage Stabilized)." YouTube. December 1, 2012. https://www.youtube.com/watch?v=Us6jo8bl2lk.

Brockenbrough, Martha. *Finding Bigfoot: Everything You Need to Know.* New York: Feiwel and Friends, 2013.

Casciato, Paul. "Police Wanted to Protect Loch Ness Monster." Reuters. April 27, 2010. http://www.reuters.com/article/us-scotland-lochness-monster-idUSTRE63Q1VU20100427.

Coleman, Loren, and James Clark. *Cryptozoology A to Z: The Encyclopedia of Loch Monsters, Sasquatch, Chupacabras, and Other Authentic Mysteries of Nature.* New York: Fireside, 1999.

Dykstra, Peter. "Bigfoot Claim a Fake, Ex-enthusiast Says." CNN. August 19, 2008. http://www.cnn.com/2008/US/08/19/bigfoot.hoax/index.html?eref=onion.

Eberhart, George M. *Mysterious Creatures: A Guide to Cryptozoology.* Santa Barbara, CA: ABC-CLIO, 2002.

Gerhard, Ken. *A Menagerie of Mysterious BeastsL Encounters with Cryptid Creatures*. Woodbury, MN: Llewellyn Publications, 2016.

Godfrey, Linda. *American Monsters: A History of Monster Lore, Legends, and Sightings in America*. New York: Penguin Group, 2014.

————. *Monsters Among Us: An Exploration of Otherworldly Bigfoots, Wolfmen, Portals, Phantoms, and Odd Phenomena*. New York: Tarcher, 2016.

Lyons, Stephen. "The Legend of Loch Ness." PBS: NOVA. January 12, 1999. http://www.pbs.org/wgbh/nova/ancient/legend-loch-ness.html.

Martin, Douglas. "Robert Rines, Inventor and Monster Hunter, Dies at 87." *New York Times*. November 7, 2009. http://www.nytimes.com/2009/11/08/us/08rines.html.

Redfern, Nick. *The Bigfoot Book: The Encyclopedia of Sasquatch, Yeti and Cryptid Primates*. Canton, MI: Visible Ink Press, 2016.

————. *Nessie: Exploring the Supernatural Origins of the Loch Ness Monster*. Woodbury, MN: Llewellyn Publications, 2016.

Robinson, Jessica. "Northwest Professor Turns to Drones in Quest for Sasquatch." NW News Network. April 26, 2013. http://nwnewsnetwork.org/post/northwest-professor-turns-drones-quest-sasquatch.

Roosevelt, Theodore. *The Wilderness Hunter*. New York: Collier & Son, 1893.

"Zoologists in the Depths with Nessie." *The Glasgow Herald*. December 20, 1968. https://news.google.com/newspapers?nid=2507&dat=19681220&id=OX9AAAAAIBAJ&sjid=waMMAAAAIBAJ&pg=3828,3632069.

INDEX

ABOUT THE AUTHOR

Matt Bougie grew up in a small town in central Wisconsin. After graduating from St. Norbert College in De Pere, he moved to Milwaukee, Wisconsin, to pursue a career. He still lives there, working at a marketing company and as a freelance writer. In his free time, he enjoys watching sports, riding his bicycle, reading, and playing with his dogs.